AVOID 11 COSTLY *Mistakes* BEFORE TAKING EV DEALERSHIP

AVOID 11 COSTLY *Mistakes* BEFORE TAKING EV DEALERSHIP

Vinod Chaudhary

Worldwide Published by
Pendown Press

PENDOWN PRESS LLP

An ISO 9001 & ISO 14001 Certified Co.,

Regd. Office: 3767A, Kanhaiya Nagar,
Tri Nagar, Delhi-110035
Ph.: 8130886000, 9650072927
E-mail: info@pendownpress.com
Branch Office: 1A/2A, 20, Hari Sadan, Ansari Road,
Daryaganj, New Delhi-110002
Ph.: 011-45794768
Website: PendownPress.com

Edition: 2024
Price: ₹ 499/-
ISBN: 978-93-6338-791-1

Layout and Cover Designed by Pendown Graphics Team
Printed and Bound in India by Thomson Press India Ltd.

TABLE OF CONTENTS

About Author

Vinod Chaudhary is a renowned automobile industry expert with an impressive 27 years of experience. His extensive career has taken him to 10 countries, where he has demonstrated exceptional leadership and sales acumen. Under his guidance, his customers have achieved remarkable sales growth, increasing from a modest 10 units per month to a staggering 70 units per month within a year.

He has led his company to great success, expanding its reach to 14 states. This growth shows his ability to plan and manage well. Under his leadership, the company has seen huge growth, with sales doubling every year for three years. In 2020, the company had a small presence in 3 states with 50 dealers. By 2023, Vinod had grown the company to have a large network of over 150 dealers across 14 states.

Vinod is an alumnus of the prestigious BITS Pilani, where he earned his Master's in Technology. He is also a sought-after guest lecturer at various engineering universities, where he shares his industry insights and knowledge with the next generation of professionals. His dedication to advancing the industry through education and practical insights has positioned him as a respected authority in both academic and professional circles.

Throughout his career, he has demonstrated a unique ability to drive sales growth, expand business presence, and foster strategic partnerships. His expertise and leadership have been instrumental in shaping the automobile industry, and his continued involvement in the sector is a testament to his enduring passion and commitment. His journey serves as an inspiration to aspiring professionals and entrepreneurs alike, illustrating the transformative power of innovation, leadership, and dedication in the automotive industry.

Introduction

A well-planned e-rickshaw business can work wonders for your business, irrespective of the industry you are in, provided it is put together in a seamless and cohesive manner.

Trust me, I speak from experience.

Hello, my name is Vinod Chaudhary, and I am a leading EV expert.

My journey with e-rickshaw marketing began early in my career as an EV expert, with 27 years of experience in the automobile industry. Since then, it has never failed to impress me, not only in terms of establishing lasting relationships with my clients but also in generating leads for my business.

I live and breathe EV marketing daily, and it continues to top my list of marketing channels that deliver measurable results consistently. Over the years, I have successfully used e-rickshaw marketing tools and techniques to build my own business. I have also helped numerous small business owners, startups, and entrepreneurs get more from their e-rickshaw marketing initiatives.

The journey so far has been brilliant!

You must be wondering why I am sharing this free eBook when I could have charged a premium for sharing the information. After all, if you implement the suggestions contained within this eBook, you can achieve significant growth for your business. Besides, as we often learn in business parlance, "there is no free lunch."

So why this free eBook?

First, being in love with e-rickshaw marketing, it breaks my heart to see how people abuse it. I want to help as many people as possible get on the right path.

Second, due to time constraints, I am unable to coach everyone personally. This book is my gift to small business owners and startups. It shares the 10 mistakes I have learnt during my journey as an EV expert.

I hope these lessons will steer you towards the path of success in the e-rickshaw business.

So, without further ado, let's explore these 10 costly mistakes.

Warm Regards,

Vinod Chaudhary

Acknowledgement

Dear Readers,

I am grateful for the opportunity to share my experiences and insights with you. This book represents a compilation of years of experience, learning, and growth. I hope that the words within these pages inspire, inform, and resonate with each reader, regardless of their background or familiarity with the subject matter.

I am deeply grateful to the wonderful individuals who have played instrumental roles in shaping my journey and contributing to my achievements.

To my parents, you have always believed in me. I'm so grateful for everything you've done.

My wife, Rachna, you are not just my partner but the foundation of my strength. I couldn't have done this without your love and patience.

Aditya, Radhika, Aarohi, my wonderful children, your laughter and joy infuse my days with purpose and motivation. You inspire me to reach for the stars.

My mentor, Akshar Yadav, your guidance and wisdom have shaped me into the person I am today. I owe much of my success to your invaluable mentorship.

To all mentioned and those not named, your contributions have been crucial to my journey. Together, we have built something extraordinary, and I look forward to the continued journey of growth and success with each one of you.

Thank you for being a part of this shared experience.

Why This Book?

As a seasoned expert in the electric vehicle (EV) industry, I've witnessed many dealers struggle to succeed in their business ventures. It's a reality that hits close to home, and I'm determined to make a difference. That's why I'm writing this book - to empower EV dealers with the knowledge and strategies they need to thrive in this rapidly growing market.

Reasons:

- **Ensuring Success:** I'm committed to helping every EV dealer avoid the pitfalls of business failure, so they can build a prosperous and sustainable future.
- **Financial Security:** My goal is to equip dealers with the tools to minimize financial losses and maximize profits, ensuring a stable and secure financial foundation.
- **Empowering Entrepreneurs:** I want to support individuals who are transitioning from a job to a business, providing them with the guidance they need to navigate this critical transition and achieve long-term success.
- **Risk-Free Business:** By sharing my expertise, I aim to provide dealers with a safety net, ensuring that they're protected from financial losses even if their business venture doesn't succeed as planned.

With this book, I aim to ignite hope, inspire resilience, and pave the way for a brighter future for all entrepreneurs.

Why Should You Read This Book?

Are you ready to unlock the secrets of success in the electric vehicle industry? Then, embark on this journey with me, and discover the transformative power of knowledge. Here are the five compelling reasons why you should read this book:

- Gain Deep Insights into the EV Business
- Make Informed Decisions
- Stay Ahead with Modern Technology
- Protect Your Investments
- Preventative Business Diagnosis

By reading this book, you'll unlock the doors to a brighter future, filled with growth, prosperity, and unparalleled success in the electric vehicle industry."

The World of E-Rickshaws

The E-Rickshaw industry encompasses the manufacturing, distribution, and operation of electric rickshaws and E - loaders. Electric rickshaws, commonly known as E-Rickshaws or E-Auto Rickshaws, are three-wheeled vehicles powered by electric motors, primarily designed for short-distance urban transportation.

Key Components and Characteristics

- **Chassis:** The structural frame of the vehicle.
- **Electric Motor:** The propulsion system powered by electricity.
- **Battery:** A rechargeable energy storage unit that powers the electric motor.
- **Passenger Compartment:** The seating area for passengers, which can vary in design and capacity.
- **Three-Wheel Configuration:** Most E-Rickshaws have a three-wheel design for stability.

Market Dynamics

- **Growing Demand:** The industry has experienced a surge in demand due to concerns about air pollution, a shift toward sustainable transportation for passengers and loading, and government incentives for electric vehicles.

- **Urban Mobility:** E-Rickshaws are commonly used for short-distance travel in crowded urban areas due to their compact size.
- **Affordability:** E-Rickshaws are considered cost-effective for both manufacturers and consumers, contributing to their popularity in certain markets.

Regulatory Environment

- **Safety Standards:** Governments often impose safety regulations to ensure the reliability and safety of E-Rickshaws for both passengers and drivers.
- **Emission Regulations:** Many regions implement emissions standards to promote cleaner transportation and reduce air pollution.
- **Licensing and Registration:** Regulatory bodies typically require proper licensing for E-Rickshaw drivers and registration of vehicles to ensure compliance with legal standards.

Challenges and Opportunities

- **Challenges:** The industry faces challenges such as competition from traditional rickshaws and auto-rickshaws, infrastructure limitations, and navigating complex regulatory landscapes.
- **Opportunities:** Advancements in technology, government incentives, and expanding market reach into untapped

regions present exceptional growth opportunities. E-Rickshaws are supportive replacements for manual rickshaws and carts for material movement.

- **Global Perspective:** The E-Rickshaw industry is not limited to a specific geographical region; it has gained recognition globally. Various countries have adopted E-Rickshaws as part of their efforts to promote clean and sustainable urban transportation.

Future Trends

- **Technological Advancements:** Ongoing developments in battery technology and electric propulsion systems are expected to enhance the performance and range of E-Rickshaws.
- **Sustainability Initiatives:** Increasing awareness of environmental issues is likely to drive further adoption of E-Rickshaws as a green and sustainable mode of transportation.
- **Government Support:** Continued government support, including financial incentives and infrastructure development (e.g., free registration in regions like UP), further boosts the industry.

How I Entered the EV Industry: Personal Insights

I am driven by a deep desire to contribute to society by creating job opportunities and fostering happy families. This motivation inspires me to work tirelessly for the betterment of society.

I began my journey by establishing my own dealership and running it successfully. Concurrently, I started purchasing chassis and kits from the market. During this time, I had the privilege of meeting Mr. Sarvesh Batra, a pioneer in the EV industry and the owner of CY International (CY GOLD). Spending four hours with him was invaluable as he provided guidance at every step.

I assembled two e-rickshaws, obtained a license from an ICAT holder, and sold these vehicles in the market. But during that time, when I was assembling them in another person's factory, I started questioning myself—what was I really doing here, and what kind of place was this? There was no care for my e-rickshaw kit, and the company didn't have a proper system for manufacturing e-rickshaws.

On the other hand, I had orders from the market, so I decided to start my own business in a 1500 Sq. feet area. From there, I began my venture. However, I didn't have government approval to sell. You know that when you have clarity in business and a clear direction, God is with you. Suddenly, I came to know that someone was selling their e-rickshaw business, and I saw an opportunity to buy the ICAT certificate and basic assets from them.

But here, I faced a problem: I struggled with how to make a payment to him, and one of the three businessmen I was in contact with told me that he would infuse money for me to start. However, he backed out, leaving me in a difficult situation after I had already made an agreement with that company and given them an advance payment.

Now I had no choice but to move forward with my decision. Then my friend Harbir gave me unconditional financial support, and I moved forward with this. Today, the company is running in a 36,000-square-foot premises.

I received great support from my wife, who stood by me at every step, and my son, who always boosted my morale.

These are the reasons that motivated me to start this business.

Vinod Chaudhary

Mistake 1

Not Knowing About Their Facilities

> *Knowing your manufacturer's facilities is like knowing the roadmap to your own success.*
>
> ***- Anonymous***

When entering the e-rickshaw business, it's common to select a manufacturer based solely on feedback from sales teams or others, without knowing much about the actual manufacturer. Sometimes, a single visit to their facilities determines your decision to buy from them or not.

Is this the right approach?

There are crucial aspects you should consider about the manufacturer:

➢ **Sourcing and Supply Chain**

- Understanding where the manufacturer sources their raw materials and components from is essential. A reliable and ethical supply chain ensures consistent quality and availability of parts, minimizing delays and maintaining product standards. Assessing their suppliers' credibility and the stability of their supply chain can provide insights into the reliability and longevity of the e-rickshaw manufacturer.

- **Manufacturing Process**
  - The efficiency and sophistication of the manufacturing process significantly impact the quality and durability of the e-rickshaws. Look for manufacturers with modern, automated production lines that adhere to industry best practices and quality control standards. This ensures that each vehicle is built with precision and uniformity, reducing the likelihood of defects and increasing overall performance.
- **CED Coating, Liquid Painting, Powder Coating**
  - The methods used for coating and painting the e-rickshaws play a vital role in their durability and resistance to environmental factors. CED (Cathodic Electrodeposition) coating, liquid painting, and powder coating are advanced techniques that provide superior corrosion resistance and aesthetic appeal. A manufacturer that invests in these technologies demonstrates a commitment to producing long-lasting and visually appealing vehicles.
- **Assembly Line**
  - The organization and efficiency of the assembly line can greatly affect the final product's quality and consistency. A well-structured assembly line with skilled workers and strict quality control measures ensures that each e-rickshaw meets high standards. Observing the assembly process can give you confidence in the manufacturer's ability to deliver reliable and well-constructed vehicles.

- **Packing**
  - Proper packing is crucial to prevent damage during transportation and ensure the e-rickshaw arrives in pristine condition. Manufacturers who prioritize secure and effective packing methods demonstrate their commitment to quality from production to delivery. Investigate their packing procedures to ensure your e-rickshaw investment is protected during transit.

By thoroughly evaluating these aspects, you can make a more informed decision when selecting an e-rickshaw manufacturer. This due diligence can save you from potential issues and ensure that you partner with a reliable and high-quality manufacturer.

Case Study

Recently, a dealer visited us to see our facilities. He thought GARUD was asking him repeatedly to visit our facilities, so he decided to visit us instead. After that, he started requesting me to visit his company.

Dealer: Initially, I wasn't interested in visiting, as no other manufacturer had asked to inspect their facilities, and I was doubtful why the Elite Auto Team was requesting a visit again and again.

However, my visit to Elite Auto turned out to be enlightening. I was impressed by the quality of their raw materials and their sourcing process. Elite Auto procures raw materials from renowned companies like TATA, APOLLO, SAIL Jindal, and others, which are among the best in India. They also have a dedicated department for sourcing high-quality products from world-class manufacturers like Schindler, TVS, Eastman, CY Gold, CEAT, and Swiss. This commitment to using top-notch materials and components indicates a strong focus on quality.

Upon observing their manufacturing process, I noted the use of modern equipment such as CNC cutting machines for pipe cutting and laser and plasma machines for sheet cutting, ensuring precision and long-term product integrity. Elite Auto also excels in painting facilities, applying a double coat for powder coating and utilizing CED (Cathodic Electro Deposition) coating for rust protection. Their assembly process on a conveyor line, using the latest pneumatic tools, ensures no items are missed and guarantees efficient assembly.

Additionally, Elite Auto recognizes the importance of proper packaging. Unlike many EV manufacturers who consider packaging a waste of money, Elite Auto uses thick and durable materials to safeguard their products during transit. This attention to detail, from sourcing to final packaging, highlights Elite Auto's dedication to delivering superior e-rickshaws. This visit not only dispelled my doubts but also underscored the importance of thoroughly evaluating manufacturers' facilities to understand their commitment to quality and excellence.

Even with impressive manufacturing facilities, market feedback remains crucial in choosing the right manufacturer. In the next chapter, we'll explore how marketing feedback impacts your business decisions.

Mistake 2

Market Feedback

> *The aim of marketing is to know and understand the customer so well the product or service fits him and sells itself.*
>
> **- Peter Drucker**

Why is Market Feedback So Important?

I would like to emphasize this because positive market feedback regarding product quality and service indicates suitability for end customers. Conversely, negative feedback suggests the product may not be suitable for dealers. Market feedback encompasses more than just product performance; it also includes after-sales service, company response, the profit generated from sales, and the overall impact on the customer's life after associating with you.

Having market feedback from dealers and end customers helps in making informed decisions promptly.

When gathering market feedback from manufacturers, consider the following:

- **Who are your dealers?**
  - Understand the profile and background of your dealers.
- **Where are they located?**
  - Geographical location can impact market dynamics and feedback.

- **What are their monthly sales figures?**
  - Sales data can provide insights into product performance and market acceptance.
- **How long have they been associated with the manufacturer?**
  - Longevity of the relationship indicates satisfaction and reliability.
- **Why have they chosen to stay with this company despite other options?**
  - Reasons for loyalty can highlight the manufacturer's strengths.
- **What benefits do they derive from the manufacturer?**
  - Identifying the specific advantages can help in refining the product and service offerings.

Case studies and testimonials can demonstrate customer satisfaction and the benefits derived from quality products and services. This feedback loop is essential for continuous improvement and maintaining a competitive edge in the market.

Case Study

I'd like to highlight one of our dealers based in Shahjahanpur, who joined us in September 2022. Initially, he was hesitant to associate with us as a dealership, and despite not having visited our facilities yet, he has successfully sold over 500 vehicles in just one year. Typically, EV dealers invest lakhs of money in obtaining a dealership, without receiving warranties on time, sales, and service. While the initial investment is a one-time expense, the benefits of sales, service, and warranty last a lifetime.

COMPANY PRESENCE IN INDIA

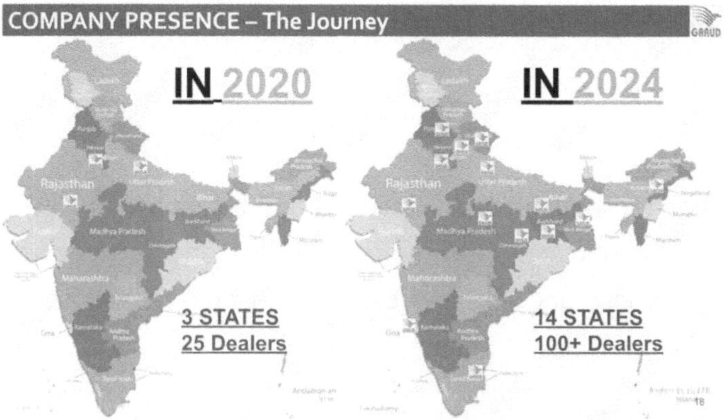

PARTNERSHIP WITH GARUD

5 सितंबर, 2022 को शुरू हुई गरुड़ के साथ हमारी साझेदारी ने 500 से अधिक ई-रिक्शा की बिक्री के साथ कुल 5 करोड़ 76 लाख का कारोबार किया है, हमारा सहयोग बाजार की वृद्धि और सफलता को बढ़ावा देने वाले एक फलदायी उद्यम को दर्शाता है।

TESTIMONIAL

ELITE AUTO एरिया मैनेजर व्यवसाय विकास के लिए हमारा समर्थन कर रहा है |
जिसका कारण हम आज 4 जिले में काम कर रहे हैं।

पहले 20 गाड़ी बचते थे आज 60 गाड़ी बचते हैं

Sidharth Shukla
Annapurna Agency,
Shahjanpur UP

Don't you think this aspect needs attention? In the next chapter, we'll discuss how warranty, sales, and services impact your business and life, and explore the best market solutions for this.

Mistake 3

After Sales and Service - The Backbone of the Industry

> *After-sales service isn't just a department; it's the heartbeat of our commitment to customers.*
>
> **- Anonymous**

Why are warranty, after sales, and service the backbone of any industry?

It's essential to understand that if a manufacturer provides timely after sales and service, no one can fail in the industry.

Rate negotiation and pricing are one-time tasks, but without after sales and service, you'll incur significant losses. Before finalizing a manufacturer, consider the following points:

- Company's customer warranty register
- Warranty duration
- Warranty policy coverage - Does it cover the entire product?
- Specific warranty periods for each product

Why Warranty?

- **Customer Confidence:** Offering a warranty instills confidence in consumers regarding the quality and reliability of a product.

- **Quality Assurance:** By providing a warranty, a company demonstrates confidence in the product's quality, signaling reliability and durability.
- **Risk Reduction for Consumers:** Purchasing products involves a degree of risk for consumers. A warranty reduces this risk by assuring customers that the manufacturer will repair or replace any malfunctioning product within a specified period, at no additional cost.
- **Competitive Advantages:** A robust warranty policy and extended warranty periods make products more appealing to consumers, leading to increased sales for both the manufacturer and dealers.
- **Trust building:** Excellent customer service through warranties fosters customer loyalty, builds trust, and nurtures positive relationships. This can result in repeat business and positive word-of-mouth referrals.
- **Long-Term Cost Savings for Customers:** While manufacturers incur costs associated with honoring warranties, consumers benefit by potentially avoiding repair or replacement costs during the warranty period. This can lead to long-term cost savings for the consumer.
- **Product Improvement Feedback:** Honoring warranties provides valuable data on product failures and defects, contributing to ongoing product quality enhancement.
- **Brand Reputation:** A company's reputation is closely tied to the quality of its products and how well it supports customers. A warranty that is honored promptly and

efficiently enhances the brand's reputation for reliability and customer satisfaction.

Case Study

We have a dealer in Raipur, Chhattisgarh. Initially, we were concerned about the warranty since he was approximately 1200 Km away from us, and spare parts facilities were scarce in his state. In fact, his city rarely had any facilities for e-rickshaw spare parts, making them entirely dependent on the manufacturer. Previously, he was associated with one of India's top 5 manufacturers before joining us. However, he didn't receive timely after-sales and service, prompting him to switch manufacturers.

After delivering the first batch to him, he received warranty coverage for one item after three months. He decided to associate with us after visiting our facilities, where we proposed the following service warranties:

- Our 24-hour warranty service provided him with significant relief.
- We included additional spare parts in the first delivery batch, enabling him to service his customers within an hour.
- In India, we officially declare the following warranties at Elite Auto:
    - 6 months warranty on everything
    - 12 months warranty on motor and controller
    - 24 months warranty on charger
    - 36 months warranty on chassis

- Upto 24 months warranty on LED battery
- 36 months warranty on Lithium battery

TESTIMONIAL

Elite Auto की **24 घंटे की रिटर्न वारंटी पॉलिसी** ने मेरे लिए वरदान साबित हुआ है जिसकी कीमत कभी नहीं मापी जा सकती है .

Zero to 20 Nos per month only in 3 month time.

CUSTOMER SATISFACTION - 100%

Adarsh Singh
A.K. Motors
Raipur - Chattisgarh

47

Yes, warranty plays a very important role in the EV business. When a manufacturer provides a warranty, the customer is protected from financial impacts, as they can rely on the manufacturer's support. Would you be interested in purchasing an inferior product that breaks down frequently? Definitely not. You need a reliable product that doesn't break down often. In this regard, product quality plays a very crucial role in your business.

In the next chapter, we will discuss how product quality is the most important aspect of any product.

Mistake 4

Product Quality

> *Quality means doing it right when no one is looking.*
>
> **- Henry Ford**

Why does everyone talk about product quality? Do you think product quality is very important to everyone?

Let me tell you, if you have a GREAT product, you won't need to worry about many things in business, and your business will never fail.

Customer Satisfaction

High-quality e-rickshaws contribute significantly to customer satisfaction. Strong, reliable vehicles enhance the overall experience for passengers and operators, leading to positive reviews and repeat business.

Durability and Longevity

The best quality e-rickshaws are designed to be more durable and have a longer lifespan. This reduces the frequency of breakdowns and repair needs, minimizing downtime for operators and improving the overall cost-effectiveness of running the business.

Safety

High-quality standards are directly tied to safety standards. Robust e-rickshaws are more likely to meet safety regulations, ensuring a secure mode of transportation for passengers and reducing the risk of accidents or malfunctions.

Reduced Maintenance Costs

Well-constructed e-rickshaws often require less maintenance. Components made from quality materials and craftsmanship are less prone to wear and tear, thereby reducing overall maintenance costs for the e-rickshaw business.

Brand Reputation

The quality of e-rickshaws significantly impacts the brand reputation of the manufacturer and the e-rickshaw business as a whole. A positive reputation for reliable, high-quality vehicles attracts more customers and builds trust in the market.

Compliance with Regulations

High-quality e-rickshaws are more likely to comply with environmental and safety regulations. Compliance with these standards is essential for the legal operation of the business, helping to avoid fines and legal complications.

Operational Efficiency

Quality e-rickshaws often come equipped with efficient and advanced features like ZERO EARTHING. This can improve the overall operational efficiency of the business, including factors such as energy efficiency, better battery life, and improved performance.

Resale Value

Maintaining quality over time increases the resale value of e-rickshaws. This can be beneficial if the business decides to upgrade its fleet or sell vehicles after a certain period.

Customer Loyalty:

Consistently providing high-quality e-rickshaws builds customer loyalty. Satisfied operators are more likely to continue purchasing vehicles from the same manufacturer, fostering long-term relationships and repeat business.

Competitive Advantage:

In a competitive market, offering high-quality e-rickshaws gives a significant edge. It positions the business as a reliable and trustworthy choice, attracting customers who prioritize quality and reliability.

While selecting a product, you need to consider product quality in following ways:

- What is their product warranty period?
- Where do they source their raw materials? If raw materials are sourced locally, the product may also be local in quality.
- The manufacturing process plays a very important role in product quality.
- Checkpoints during manufacturing.

- Final Dispatch Checklist - Do they include a final dispatch checklist with every shipment?

These are basic checkpoints for assessing product quality. There are many other points that should be checked with manufacturers.

Case Study

One of our dealers in Assam was concerned about product quality. During the COVID-19 pandemic, he inspected our raw material supplies and found that we sourced them from India's top supplier. This assurance led him to partner with us and establish his business in Assam. As the proverb goes, 'Timely food, even if less than expected, is essential for survival and longevity.' Similarly, delivery plays a vital role in business; on-time delivery is crucial.

TESTIMONIAL

GARUD

I was in doubt that how startup company maintain the best quality product in Covid time. Who is their raw material source. I asked from my Brother based in Faridabad and in Steel business.
I was wrong when my brother found that Elite auto is buying the raw material from India's number - 1 manufacturers like Apollo , TATA , Jindal , SAIL.
Based on this i took the distributorship for Assam and now very Happy from the product quality

Sanjay Agarwal
Poly Product
Guwahati- Assam

If you can deliver products promptly, nothing else matters. Therefore, ON-TIME DELIVERY is extremely important for any business. In the next chapter, we'll explore how delivery impacts your business.

Mistake 5

On-Time Delivery

> *In a world of choices, on-time delivery is our promise, and customer satisfaction is our reward.*
>
> **- Vinod Chaudhary**

A manufacturer may have

- Excellent facilities.
- Top-notch quality.
- Superb sales and services.

But if they do not deliver on time, do you think this kind of service will help you grow your business significantly?

Think again and again for this before finalizing the dealership with any manufacturer.

Elite Auto's commitment to 48-hour dispatches helps our customers in the following ways

- Reduce their risk for sales failure.
- Lowering inventory levels.
- Avoiding dead stock, which saves money.

How We Achieve This:

- Our sales team takes weekly and monthly plans from each and every customer.

- Elite Auto supports our customers' sales plan.
- We help them create inventory plans based on their sales projections.

Timely Delivery

Ensure that deliveries are made promptly and within the promised timeframe. Customers appreciate punctuality, especially when they're expecting their orders to arrive at a certain time.

Transit Insurance

Ensure transit insurance for each and every vehicle dispatched, improving dealer financial security and ensuring safe delivery to their destination. This covers accidents, theft, and other potential issues.

Communication

Keep lines of communication open with your customers. Send them notifications or updates regarding their delivery status, such as when the order has been dispatched and when it's out for delivery. This helps manage expectations .

Safe and Secure Handling

Ensure that items being delivered are handled with care to prevent damage or breakage during transit. Invest in proper packaging materials and train your delivery personnel in safe handling practices.

Customer Feedback and Support

Encourage customers to provide feedback on their delivery experience and use that feedback to improve your services continuously. Additionally, offer responsive customer support to address any issues or concerns promptly.

Technology Integration

Leverage technology to streamline the delivery process further. Implement GPS tracking systems to allow customers to track their orders in real-time.

Customer Service

Provide excellent customer service at every stage of the delivery process. Train your delivery personnel to be polite, helpful, and responsive to customer inquiries or concerns. A positive interaction can significantly enhance the customer experience.

Case Study

One of our dealers in Haryana, Mr. Manish from Gurgaon, was concerned about E-Cart delivery since some products were customized for specific customers.

When he discussed delivery with us and saw our delivery monitoring system, he was delighted. His previous experience working in many MNCs and large corporations made him a systematic entrepreneur. His confidence in our facilities, delivery times, and our customized E-Carts helped him double his business within six months.

He expanded with two additional dealerships in his area and explored new territories to serve more customers.

Receiving vehicles on time is crucial. If you can't outperform your competition, there's no satisfaction in purchasing or conducting EV business.

In the next chapter, we'll explore how to outperform your competition.

Mistake 6

High Competition

> *In the business world, the rearview mirror is always clearer than the windshield.*
>
> **- Warren Buffett**

Every person worries about high competition. In fact, 57% of EV business owners are concerned about the intense competition in the market, according to a survey conducted by Elite Auto among EV business owners.

Before finalizing the manufacturer, any dealer needs to understand the kind of marketing support the manufacturer will provide to the dealer. This support can include:

- **Canopy:** Extending reach into areas without physical showrooms, enabling direct customer engagement.
- **Demo vehicles:** Providing test drives gives customers more confidence and facilitates their decision-making process.
- **Service camp:** These provide additional support for products and help in cost-saving measures.
- **Leaflets and catalogs:** These help reach customers interested in buying your products, drawing them to your showroom.
- **Unique Selling Proposition (USP):** Identify what distinguishes your dealership from competitors. This could involve offering a wider range of e-rickshaw models,

providing superior after-sales service, offering financing options, or emphasizing environmentally-friendly features. Highlighting your unique advantages helps attract customers and sets you apart in a competitive market.

- **Quality Products:** Partner with reputable e-rickshaw manufacturers known for producing high-quality vehicles. Offering reliable and durable e-rickshaws enhances your reputation and builds trust with customers. Ensure that the e-rickshaws you sell meet safety standards and have excellent performance characteristics.
- **Customer Service Excellence:** Provide knowledgeable, attentive service throughout the entire sales journey. Addressing customer concerns promptly and exceeding expectations fosters long-term customer loyalty.
- **Marketing and Branding:** Develop a strong brand identity and market your dealership effectively, utilizing online and offline channels to reach potential customers, including social media, Indiamart, local advertising, and participation in industry events. Highlight your USP and customer testimonials to build credibility and attract buyers.
- **Value-added Services:** Offer additional services that enhance the customer experience and provide added value. This could include vehicle customization options, maintenance packages, training programs for drivers. Providing comprehensive solutions beyond product sales enhances customer satisfaction and distinguishes the dealership in the market.

and many more.

Case Study

Our Munger, Bihar dealer, Mr. Chandan, was struggling with sales and marketing difficulties in his area. Despite running his business since 2014, he had only managed to sell 10 units per month in eight years. Our field sales team and telemarketing team supported him in overcoming the competition, and our product's special features and USP gave him an additional boost. We implemented our strategy by providing double engine support, combining telemarketing and field team efforts. His business grew rapidly, increasing sales significantly within just three months. This demonstrates how to outdo your competition, but it's crucial to remember that without proper after-sales and service care, sustaining your business won't be possible. Therefore, customer care is extremely important for business sustainability. In the next chapter, we will discuss customer service and care in detail.

Mistake 7

Customer Care

> *Customers may forget what you said but they'll never forget how you made them feel.*
>
> **- Anonymous**

You may find big facilities and good quality products, but if there's no one to listen to your concerns or offer support when needed most, it can be frustrating. Dealers often make the mistake of finalizing partnerships without thoroughly assessing whether the manufacturer provides sufficient customer care facilities.

Consider this analogy: Do you care for your baby, or do you care for your parents? Similarly, do you have a caretaker for your business? Having a caretaker for your business means you don't have to worry about losses. Big companies always have customer care facilities, and their growth depends on the kind of care they provide.

Benefits of Excellent Customer Care

- **Enhanced Customer Satisfaction:** Prompt and effective customer support ensures timely resolution of issues, leading to higher customer satisfaction. Customers feel valued and supported throughout their interactions with the business.

- **Repeat Business and Loyalty:** Excellent customer care builds trust and loyalty. Satisfied customers are more likely to return for future purchases or services, contributing to long-term business growth.
- **Positive Reputation and Word-of-Mouth:** Satisfied customers are likely to share their positive experiences with others, leading to positive word-of-mouth referrals. A reputation for excellent customer care can attract new customers to the e-rickshaw business, contributing to its growth and expansion in the market.
- **Differentiation from Competitors:** In a competitive market, superior customer care can be a key differentiator for an e-rickshaw business. By consistently delivering exceptional customer support, the business sets itself apart from competitors and establishes a reputation for reliability and responsiveness.
- **Feedback for Improvement:** Customer care interactions provide valuable feedback that can be used to identify areas for improvement in products, services, and processes. By listening to customer concerns and suggestions, the business can make necessary adjustments to enhance the overall customer experience and drive growth.
- **Upselling and Cross-Selling Opportunities:** Customer care interactions present opportunities to upsell or cross-sell additional products or services. Well-trained customer care representatives can identify customer needs and preferences, recommend relevant upgrades or accessories, and capitalize on opportunities to increase sales revenue.

Leveraging these opportunities contributes to the overall growth and profitability of your e-rickshaw business.

Engineers should serve as caretakers, addressing all concerns and problems from a central point. In the e-rickshaw business, 80% of manufacturers focus primarily on sales rather than professional customer care. Upon entering this industry, I realized that effective customer care is crucial for business support and growth.

It's universally acknowledged that everyone requires care. Establishing a customer care center can promptly support dealers and provide optimal solutions within a short period.

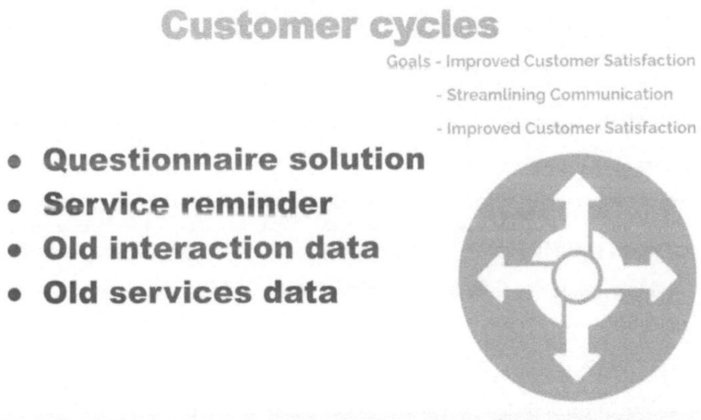

Customer care not only enables you to support your customers but also plays a critical role in facilitating sales. Lack of financing can hinder your ability to sell products in large quantities. However, we also understand that financing is a crucial aspect, as lack of finance can hinder sales. In the next chapter, we will explore finance facilities in more detail.

Case Study

One of our dealers from Ambala, Punjab was struggling to increase his business. Then, he contacted me, and we had a discussion about the issues he was facing. I suggested several solutions that could help him grow his business. One of those suggestions was to arrange a meeting with existing customers. And he did exactly that. He arranged a meeting with his existing customers, offered them coffee and snacks, listened to their concerns about the rickshaws, and provided instant solutions. He also gave gifts to customers who had purchased two or more rickshaws from us. And guess what? It really worked! He received an order for 12 E-Rickshaws in a single day. Now, it's been almost three months since they've been organizing such meetings with almost 70 customers at regular intervals, and as a result, they are reaping good profits, earning trust, and gaining respect.

Case Study .. Universal Auto

- मैं अंबाला शहर में बिक्री के लिए संघर्ष कर रहा था। जब मैंने विनोद जी से चर्चा की , कि बिक्री कैसे सुधारी जाए। फिर विनोद जी ने बिक्री में तुरंत सुधार लाने के लिए मुझसे बहुत सारे विचारों पर चर्चा की।
- हमने क्या किया था ?
- हमने अपनी ओर से दिनांक 26th April'24 एक ग्राहक बैठक आयोजित की।
- हम लगभग 70 ग्राहकों से मिलते हैं और इन ग्राहकों को प्यार से चाय और नाश्ता देते हैं, उनकी सभी चिंताओं का तुरंत समाधान करते हैं और उन ग्राहकों को उपहार देते हैं जिन्होंने 2 या अधिक रिक्शा लिए थे।
- नतीजा :
- एक ही दिन 12 ई रिक्शा की बुकिंग मिल गयी.

28

ग्राहक से मन की बात
गरुड़ के साथ

UNIVERSAL AUTOMOBILES
GARUD

Mistake 8

Finance Facilities

It's not how much money you make, but how much money you keep, how hard it works for you, and how many generations you keep it for.

- Robert Kiyosaki

As you know, e-rickshaw sales lack adequate finance facilities. Government banks and nationalized banks do not support e-rickshaw manufacturers and dealers, assuming owners cannot provide timely EMIs. This assumption was true about six years ago, with a 10% NPA (Non-Performing Asset) rate when government banks offered finance facilities. At that time, e-rickshaw customers were not financially stable, and e-rickshaws were not popular for last-mile connectivity.

Initially, we faced this problem and struggled to find dealers who could secure financing for their customers. However, after collaborating with NBFCs (Non-Banking Financial Companies) and government banks, signing MOUs at the state and national levels, our business and our dealers' business doubled within four to six months.

A crucial aspect of the strategy is understanding the specific needs and financial behaviors of e-rickshaw customers. By tailoring finance products to better suit their income patterns and payment capabilities, businesses can offer more flexible and accessible financing options. This includes lower down payments, longer loan tenures, and competitive interest rates, making e-rickshaws more affordable for a broader customer base.

Advocating for policy changes and working closely with regulatory bodies to improve the overall financial ecosystem for e-rickshaws can also be beneficial. By demonstrating the viability and growth potential of the e-rickshaw market, businesses can encourage more financial institutions to participate, thereby expanding the available funding options.

We analyzed the problem in detail and found that resolving it would rapidly increase our business.

We partnered with over 10 financial institutions to facilitate growth for both their and our businesses.

FINANCIAL TIE UP - Financial Tie UP with financial institutes

By thoroughly analyzing the problem and seeking practical solutions, addressing the financing issue is key to expanding operations. Partnering with multiple financial institutions creates opportunities for growth and stability in the e-rickshaw market. This multi-faceted approach not only strengthens businesses but also contributes to the broader adoption of e-rickshaws as a sustainable and economical mode of transportation.

Case Study

Our business partner, based in Shahjahanpur, was facing a significant challenge in financing for his customers. Despite his best efforts, he struggled to find a reliable financing solution that could provide timely support to his clients. This issue was hindering his business growth and causing frustration among his customers.

Determined to find a solution, we stepped in and negotiated an agreement with a reputable NBFC (Non-Banking Financial Company) specifically for his area. This partnership enabled us to offer a streamlined financing process, ensuring payment disbursement within 24 hours of receiving scanned documents from the finance company.

With this new financing solution in place, our business partner in Shahjahanpur witnessed a remarkable transformation. His customers could now access timely financing, and his business began to flourish. The swift payment disbursement process eliminated the previous hurdles, allowing him to focus on growing his business with confidence.

Thanks to our collaboration with the NBFC, our partner's customers could now enjoy hassle-free financing, and his business experienced a significant boost. This success story showcases the power of strategic partnerships in addressing financial challenges and driving business growth.

Mistake 9

Training and Technical Assistance

> *Tell me and I forget. Teach me and I remember. Involve me and I learn.*
>
> **- Benjamin Franklin**

Do you think your business will grow without training your sales team and e-rickshaw mechanics?

- **Sales Training:** This will help increase sales exponentially. A trained sales team can make selling easier, as they will complete 50-80% of the customer readiness process, leaving the owner to finalize prices and prepare for delivery. This enables the owner to focus on building relationships.
- **Mechanic Training:** This increases customer satisfaction, leading to happy customers who will refer friends and relatives, effectively doing marketing for you. With referrals, the sales process becomes easier.

The benefits of training are:

- **Sales Training:**
    - Boosts sales
    - Makes selling easier
    - Enables owners to focus on relationship building

- **Mechanic Training:**
  - Increases customer satisfaction
  - Encourages customer referrals
  - Simplifies the sales process

In conclusion, investing in training for both sales and mechanics not only enhances operational efficiency but also boosts customer satisfaction and facilitates business growth.

Case Study

We partnered with a dealer in Lucknow who had been running a TVS two-wheeler business for 11 years. He was confident that his mechanic and he could handle the EV business without training or company support. However, he underestimated the differences between EV customers and two-wheeler customers. Unlike personal use two-wheelers, EV rickshaws and e-carts are used commercially, generating daily income and relying on battery capacity.

Once he started his EV business, he encountered various difficulties with customers. He approached us for help, and Elite Auto provided training for his sales team, mechanics, and business owners. The entire team visited our factory for comprehensive, free training.

After receiving this training, he was able to run his business smoothly.

Mistake 10

Diagnosis Before Starting an EV Business

Adaptability, innovation, and perseverance are the keys to navigating its dynamic landscape.

- Anonymous

When someone considers starting or running an EV business, they typically fall into one of five levels of awareness:

- Not aware
- Aware
- Fully aware
- Product aware
- Problem aware

Every business owner initiates their venture based on their level of awareness. Unfortunately, 80% of business owners incur significant losses due to insufficient or incomplete knowledge, often without adequate guidance before starting their ventures. Similar to the stock market where 90% of people fail due to investing with insufficient knowledge, starting an EV business without adequate understanding can lead to similar outcomes.

Before embarking on this journey, conducting a thorough diagnosis of your readiness and the market conditions is crucial. This includes understanding regulatory requirements, potential subsidies or incentives, technological advancements, and consumer preferences. It's essential to assess your financial capabilities and prepare for unexpected challenges, as the EV industry is marked by rapid changes and intense competition.

Engaging with industry experts, attending relevant workshops, and conducting comprehensive market research can significantly enhance your understanding and preparedness. By investing time and resources in gaining a deep insight into the EV sector, you can identify potential pitfalls and develop strategies to mitigate risks. Remember, a well-informed and meticulously planned approach can significantly increase your chances of success in the dynamic and evolving landscape of the EV business.

At Elite Auto, we understand the importance of diagnosis. Our team analyzes the needs of customers with zero knowledge and conducts business analysis accordingly. Unlike other companies in India, we offer free diagnosis services, even if the customer doesn't intend to do business with us. Our diagnosis team provides a thorough business analysis before entering the EV business, guiding customers on the right track and advising against unsuitable ventures, regardless of their financial resources.

Mistake 11

Poor Location and Accessibility

Picking the wrong place for your EV dealership can be a big setback. It might be hard for people to see your store, getting there could be a hassle, and you might not be close to potential customers. This can mean fewer people visiting, fewer sales, and trouble competing with other EV dealerships. **But wait! There's a bright side!**

Even if your location isn't ideal, you can still turn things around. Here's how:

- **Find the hidden gems:** Instead of seeing a bad location as a bummer, look for hidden opportunities! Do some research to see who lives around your dealership and what they're interested in. Maybe there are eco-friendly families nearby who would love an EV, or businesses looking for sustainable ways to get around. By understanding your neighbors, you can tailor your sales pitch to what matters to them.
- **Make it easy to get to you:** Even if your location isn't the most visible, you can make it easier for people to find you. Put up clear signs, both at your dealership and around town, to point people in the right direction. Partner with nearby businesses to get the word out, or offer test drives where you bring the car to the customer! You can even have a mobile service unit that goes to customers who can't make it to you.
- **Be the best EV dealership ever:** Set yourself apart from the competition by creating an awesome customer experience, even if your location isn't perfect. Offer personalized advice, online tours, and cool online tools so people can learn about EVs from anywhere. Focus on giving great

customer service and being honest throughout the sales process. People will be more willing to travel to you if they know they'll get treated well.

- **Get involved with your community:** Become a big part of your town! Partner with local schools, organizations, or groups to get your name out there. Sponsor events, teach people about EVs, and be a leader in sustainable transportation. By getting involved, you'll build trust and get people talking about your dealership in a positive way.

  Think ahead! Stay in the loop about what's happening in your area. Is there new construction planned? Are more people moving in? Knowing what's coming can help you prepare for future customers. Position yourself as a forward-thinking business that cares about the environment, and you'll attract eco-conscious customers.

So, remember, even if your dealership isn't in the most ideal spot, it doesn't have to hold you back! By being creative, providing a great experience, and getting involved in your community, you can turn your location challenge into a big advantage! Focus on your dealership's strengths and build relationships with your neighbors to create a thriving business in the ever-changing world of EVs.

Conclusion

Before finalizing your e-rickshaw manufacturer, please ensure you check the following:

- After sales and service.
- Request proof for good service.
- Customer feedback.

EV Success Awaits!

Due to page constraints, I've only shared a glimpse of the valuable insights that can guarantee a successful decision in the EV business. If I were to write a complete book, it would span 2000 pages. I believe this book can significantly benefit your business and elevate it to new heights.

Don't wait; ensure 100% assurance with a complimentary one-on-one consultation (valued at INR 5,000). In this personalized session, I'll help you:

- **Uncover Hidden Gems**
- **Avoid Costly Losses**
- **Make Confident Decisions**

Limited Spots Available! Schedule your FREE consultation today by:

Call or WhatsApp: ***8920833353***

Scanning the QR code (for appointments):

ELITE AUTO ENGINEERS

PLOT NO. 25, GALI NO. 1, GHAZIPUR INDUSTRIAL AREA , SOHNA ROAD, FARIDABAD, HARYANA - 121005

GST NO. ***06AACCE9473E1ZL***

Location:

https://maps.google.com/?q=28.365643,77.243004

Our Offerings

Elite offers four models in their passenger vehicle lineup:

- **Prime Model:** This entry-level model offers the best-in-class running average and a sleek design. Customers prefer this model for its high running average and reliability.
- **Deluxe Model:** The Deluxe model is a robust and majestic variant, giving customers a King type feeling and a sense of pride in their purchase.
- **Butterfly Model:** The first impression of our Butterfly model is its beauty, which adds value and attracts customers. Our product combines reliability and attractiveness.

Stainless Steel

When it comes to durability, corrosion resistance, rust-free, easy cleaning, and long lifespan, our E-Rickshaws are made with stainless steel from India's number one steel manufacturer, ensuring top-notch quality.

PASSANGER

GARUD

DIVERSIFY PRODUCT PORTFOLIO

- MOTOR / CONTROLLER - 1100 Watt
- SEAT QUALITY - 1 Year
- MOTOR CONTROLLER - 1 Year
- FULL PRODUCT - 6 Month
- CHASSIS - सबसे मजबूत
- LOAD CAPACITY - 500Kg+

7

LOADER

GARUD

DIVERSIFY PRODUCT PORTFOLIO

- MOTOR / CONTROLLER - 1650 WATT
- 42" DIFFERENTIAL - नहीं पलटेगा
- DALA-4.5'X6.25'X1.5' - HIGH SPACE
- 5 PIPE CHASSIS - सबसे मजबूत
- LOAD CAPACITY - 700Kg+

8